# THE APPLE GHOST

CH00606889

# The Apple Ghost

## JOHN GLENDAY

PETERLOO POETS

First published in 1989
by Peterloo Poets
2 Kelly Gardens. Calstock. Cornwall PL18 9SA

**ISBN** 1 871471 05 2

Printed in Great Britain by
Latimer Trend & Company Ltd, Plymouth

**ACKNOWLEDGEMENTS** are due to the editors of the following journals and anthologies in whose pages some of these poems first appeared: *Behind The Lines, Blind Serpent, Chapman, The Fiddlehead, Lines Review, Observer/Arvon Prizewinners' Anthology 1985, Other Poetry, National Poetry Competition Prizewinners' Anthology 1984, New Writing Scotland 6, Poetry Matters, Radical Scotland, Scottish National Poetry Competition Anthology, Screvins, Times Literary Supplement, The Wascana Review.*

Supported by

Cornwall
County Council

WITH THE ASSISTANCE OF

SOUTH WEST ARTS

**For Penny**

# Contents

*page*

*FROM AN OCCUPIED COUNTRY*

# OTHER LIVES

# The Rise of Icarus

My father brought a German flying
helmet home from war. The summer I started
school I wore it constantly while I played

outside, or hunted through the radio
for heterodynes. He cut the hose for oxygen
when I swung it round my head at other boys.

Of course, it was too big; but I loved
the leather's warmth against my skull.
The rubber earcups hollowed out his words,

and distanced from the substance of my brain
his lectures on stealing matches, crossing roads,
or climbing haystacks in my Sunday clothes.

Once, in a dream, I pedalled a tiny plane
across our lawn; the tin propeller hoisted
me through the angled joists of air,

until the cabbages became like sprouts, then peas.
Below me, father dropped his bicycle and called
from the shadow of the house, frail as a child.

But I was much too high, too far away,
and glorying in the weightlessness of things.
So I watched him waving upwards soundlessly,

as the swelling sun beat down upon my wings.

# Flounder Fishing

1.
Without the lid on, it reminded me
Of his flat-prowed rowing boat. You'd have thought

I'd come across him dozing in the bilge's
buttoned silk. We once caught fish enough to swamp it.

A foul day. East wind. He held his face
Turned from the gusts; the taut line

Dug into a cigarette stained hand.
I leaned across, tugging against his grip

To make him jump and laugh. Later we lost
Our anchor, rode the surf towards the shore.

The wind-blown spray drifted over us,
Settling on our lips like blood.

2.
Like most keen fishers, he would not eat fish;
And those the neighbours didn't take

Flapped in an inch of water in our outhouse sink.
Later that evening, when I should have been asleep,

I crept back down to touch them; to draw blood
Upon the hidden prickles of their fins,

Then slide a finger in between the gills. Looping
The frilly garter where the hook had dragged,

I thrilled as the dying muscle gagged and pumped.
Their small, flat deaths held on to me, like love.

3.
I didn't mind the waste; it added voltage to delight.
The next day, when I placed those tile-like fishes

In the bin, I turned them belly up.
There they remained, forever smooth and shiny

In my mind—I saw them gleaming
As he sailed towards the fire—

And when I found his boat, split
Like a broom pod in the uncut grass,

I felt his fingers tugging,
Though they couldn't draw me in.

# A Dream of Gliders

Father built an airfield in the garden yesterday,
And I,
(Having ceased playing the enthusiastic child),
Laughed at him;
Told him the garden was too small.
He just pointed at the sky
Where silver wings drifted against
The bright blue air.
The hot air held them, and only held them;
Softly rocked them.
My brother caught two gliders with a magnet.

A curse on the dog in our dirty alley,
Which woke me rudely with its stupid bark;
Which dragged me back to
This building in an empty sky;
Which forced me to admit
Our garden could never have been big enough
After all.

## Distant Relations

Great Uncle Jim ran off to sea;
but he didn't sail far. He stepped

head first from his whaler, blind drunk
on rum, in a dirty squall; and sank

through the tassled carpet of God's
infinite grey room, never to be smelled again.

My Grandmother wept into her embroidery
for her brother's short, cold life;

thinking nothing of the voyage
she was doomed to make

through the mouths of worms
in a ship of grass, with her name

and times carved in the sail
no winds would bend; no gust could fill.

# In Praise Of Wireless

The dark walls
step aside.
He sees valves
glow behind their
hardboard screen
like house lights

in a distant town.
He relishes
the bitterness
of old electrons
caged in dust.
A wind from the attic

riffles the stack
of long abandoned
magazines. He searches
the frequencies for static,
wondering if some day
this same wind

might move through Berlin,
Moscow, Hilversum.
In another room,
his sleeping wife
recites the names
of dead men

she once knew.
He watches the cursor's
finger touch
each city of dull
segmented light,
and pass clean through.

# A Guided Tour

This is the house. You'll notice
how the place is overgrown; as though
his garden hoped it might contain
the stillness at its heart.

The door, remembering an impact
of policemen's boots, sways
open jaggedly with cobwebs
on its lips. This carious hall

he often crouched in, so they say,
to study far rectangular domains
where trousers marched.
These creaking stairs led to his heart,

uncarpeted. No one alive has touched
this air. Ignore the nimbuses of damp, which
sail the bare distempered walls. And this
is the famous lavatory—he often must have

watched his slackened rope of water
froth this bowl. The chipped enamel bath
displays a yellow ring of wedded age,
a golden needle's eye—he slipped

so gently through on a couple
of pegs of brandy and a razor
blade. But look. I found this
in the bedroom where the dry rot

has its lair. It's bleached
where a snail of sunlight tracked,
but you can still make out his smile,
quite fresh, although the photograph is old.

Look. This was him.

# Nightscape

It's night.
They've taken to the boats.
There's only us, adrift

On the foundering bed.
From this worn hollow
I can hear an ocean,

Beating through the hull.
The shifting surge
Erodes the heavy edges of your sleep.

It's night.
There's only us
Inside the swaying darkness

Quiet as fish;
And the sea, or someone,
Somewhere out there

Pounding and pounding and pounding
And pounding upon a door
That will never be opened.

## Aegeus

My son is coming
From over the sea.
The sea inside the woman.
The woman holding the clue of skin
Inside herself. She is also the maze;
My son is his own monster.
He must overcome the bull-headed man with goldfish eyes,
And the fish-gilled god with bull's fists,
To grow the mouth which will speak
Of a kingdom I can visit no more.
This is the wind
Which spins the gulls,
Whitens the brine,
Lifts my heart,
Swells the black sail.

# The Closed Fist Of The Exile

*for Bridget*

You crossed a floorless ocean in despair.
No stars betrayed the course; a sloppy tide
Heaved underneath the reddened moon. Astern,
The white road hissed, and darkened, and was gone.
True refugees bring nothing of the past, and so
You came, bare-handed and alone,
To a land of giants, where a stranger
With your blood spoke comfort
Through the vowels of an unknown tongue.
In sleep you frown and sigh. Your shell-whorled hands
Clasped shut against the ebbing dream,
Where an ocean softly tumbles through the dark.
A fist first built for grasping air
Takes time to learn the contours
Of the heart.

# Honesty

*Lunaria biennis*

Pale oblongs
sink their roots
into the wall;

safe behind pictures once.
We must have generated shadows
where our two lives crossed,

like nimbus clouds,
or friction
wearing wallpaper to dust.

While you arranged
dried grasses in a vase
I laid my paintbrush down,

content to watch the north light
gradually decline.
Now that's all gone.

Somehow discarded honesty survived,
cushioned in mounting dirt
beneath our walnut chest.

Hidden from scouring hoovers
with the dusty pencil,
rubber bands,

dropped pennies.
How could I have known,
as the years went drifting,

that the small change would accumulate
and the cluttered room
fill up with silence

20

like the ballast in a wall?
And who was there to tell me I would feel
your fragile silver coins

grow warm against my palm;
their only weight
the dark seed they contain?

## Remembering

A night breeze from the river
Moved through the window's skirts;
Its cool touch woke me, dreaming of your hands.
Now my cigarette smoke in the darkness
Sways like old folk's hair.
A deep time has passed.
A wide time has passed.
A dark time has passed.
A lot of water has flowed under the bed.

# *Woman With A Pale Hand*

*for my father*

winter
has pale hands
she waits in shadow
where the year hinges

holding a letter for me
her pale lips brush
against my name
already I can hear

the birds of my lungs
sing anxiously in the branches
of the ruined tree
she will surely pull them down

winter has pale thin teeth
how silently
they grow towards me
as I sleep

they are like
pegs of hyacinth
lifting the scab of earth
beneath an old man's bed

# Waiting

The gas fire bares clay teeth
In the stopped hearth.
Between its brass legs lies
A grey penumbra which the hoover cannot touch,
Where the dry rain quietly tumbles in secure neglect
Laying down endless layers of fragile polaroid.
Above all this, the old blind clock
With vexing industry swings its dull and useless axe.
And no-one comes; no-one calls.
No letter flaps a sick tongue on the mat.
No smile distorts against the misting pane.
The green phone hunched beneath its sagging weights.
Perhaps if I could say it all again . . .
But the gas fire sighs behind a hanging grin,
And the clock hacks at another stack of wood,
As the front door, in its patient wall,
Begins to heal.

# *Allotments*

Content within
your narrow acre, you will
praise the seed, the rain,
the earth and spade.

The good seed. The good
seed lifting from the earth.
The rain. The rain which
makes the earth more real.

The earth. The earth
hungry for your bootsoles.
The earth. The earth heavy
against your spade.

Your spade. Your
spade turning and turning
the year through
its dark acre.

## Incomplete Fixation

I think he looked like me
when he was young.
He said this self-portrait
was not his best, but the first
print he developed for himself.

You'll notice it was incompletely
fixed. Salts have remained
which, tarnished by the years,
have darkened the emulsion.
Permanence fell victim

to his youthful eagerness.
When he had struck his pose,
and squeezed the bulb, he trapped
an innocence which now endures
no better in the album

than the man. Nothing is truly
fixed. That which seems so,
is changing at the same rate
as ourselves. I wonder; when
he stooped to gauge the frame,

and peered out through the lens,
would he have seen
the bright inverted space
where he would stand, and from
the edges, darkness crowding in?

# The Apple Ghost

A musty smell of dampness filled the room
Where wrinkled green and yellow apples lay
On folded pages from an August newspaper.

She said:
*'My husband brought them in, you understand,*
*Only a week or two before he died.*
*He never had much truck with waste, and*
*I can't bring myself to throw them out.*
*He passed away so soon . . .'*

I understood then how the wonky kitchen door,
And the old Austin, settling upon its
Softened tyres in the wooden shed,
Were paying homage to the absence of his quiet hands.

In the late afternoon, I opened
Shallow cupboards where the sunlight leaned on
Shelf over shelf of apples, weightless with decay.
Beneath them, sheets of faded wallpaper
Showed ponies prancing through a summer field.
This must have been the only daughter's room
Before she left for good.

I did not sleep well.

The old woman told me over breakfast
How the boards were sprung in that upper hall;
But I knew I had heard his footsteps in the night,
As he dragged his wasted body to the attic room
Where the angles of the roof slide through the walls,
And the fruit lay blighted by his helpless gaze.
I knew besides that, had I crossed to the window
On the rug of moonlight,
I would have seen him down in the frosted garden,
Trying to hang the fruit back on the tree.

## Silence

Slate green,
sky grey,
and muddy umbers
of alluvial sand.

The waves have come
in their borrowed coats.

They shelve to the ocean's
imperceptible decline;
then gently fall away
like other people's lives.

Like other people's
lives, unfolding
in curves of silence,
searching for an end.

We only hear them
when they break against
our world.

# SCRIMSHAW WORK

## Scrimshaw Work

And I will flense my lines
like these, carved on the whale's
tooth through exigency or love.

And as those sailors, who once bowed
in gimballed shadows for their craft,
so I must feel the bright wake

shrivel back towards the womb—
though I would never trace that
myth, but trust instead

the swing to north, and run before
the squall; soothing with ink
the gouges in my bones.

# The Drowning Pool

This is the pool
from which
I shall not rise

water as black as love
will draw me in
water is dark

is dark
but in her eyes
turn greater darknesses

*feel how my skin*
*is white*
she whispers

*here*
*against my thighs*
and winds herself

around me
I breathe in
but she covers my mouth

my nose
my ears
my eyes

this
is the pool
in which I cannot swim

## Snow

Carefully, snow invaded,
From out of its own country,
Hidden behind the air.
All through the long night in drifting silence
The grey parachutes had come to seize my land.
Now they have turned it to their own ends,
And I am powerless but to do their will.
See how this place is made
As strange as sleep
By the enforced beauty of their gentle war.
Still, the faultless cycle will defeat them,
When their bones, once weightless starfish,
Round into allies for the slanted rain;
Though the memory of that doomed conquest will prevail
All sunlight long,
As the motes go tumbling through an empty house,
And drift to the farthest corners of my heart.

# Snow At Dachau, 1945

Frozen sidings.
Cattle trucks stand with their flanks gaping.
Starved bodies clog the doorways
Like worthless freight.
Such cold.
The breath of the survivors
Draws colour from the air.
Shuffling towards the camera, they gaze
Through the lens, and into my soul,
As though they saw vacant wagons there,
And longed to fill them.

# The Moth

If the past were an attic room
in an empty house,
though it is not;

and if memory took the form
of boxes hidden in the darkness
of the eaves; though I know

that memory is without form;
and if there were a tiny window
set in the wall of darkness;

though there is no window
and no darkness;
and if I were to feel

a moth stir, that had wings
without dust, like the skeletons
of leaves;

to struggle against
the window that is only a dream;
then I would wish

that a wish were a hand,
that a hand touched a stone,
and that stones might fly.

# Seals

Dark hair obscured your face, the tears were hidden:
*'I shall return as soon as this is over.'*
The blue keel dipped upon the ocean's fulcrum;
A pale hand moved against the superstructure.

After the wind had eased and the rains divided
Policemen with wet boots patrolled the shingle.
The fragments formed dark rings inside their Escort,
And in the pub, the juke-box music faded.

Last night I dreamed your hair lay on the pebbles;
Stroking the slime, I squeezed and burst the bladders,
Whilst in the bay, with eyeballs from dead children,
The rubber men bobbed on the silent water.

# The Widow

In the house where the smoke slides down the lum,
She watches the clock compact its tensing coils;
Reeling time back to its hidden spool, as she waits
For her drowned man to be ferried to the sea.

*"Where is the ship which will sail for the jug-lipped storm
Stern first, and the sea's warp perfect through the bow?"*
The tide shrugs shoulders, toys with a captive moon,
As the jetsam springs triumphant to the swell.

She remembers when she was old, and growing young,
While the stream climbed skywards on the brackened hill,
How she dreamed of a place where the glassy threads
Unwound to a single strand, in an unreflecting pool;

Where the butterwort shyly retracted its frail, blue face,
And the thirsty moss flourished, drawing in endless seas.

# The Weeping God Of Tiahuanaco

*"The Tiahuanaco left behind them little social impress—
only those unmistakable designs on pottery and cloth, and the cult
of the Weeping God."*
(Von Hagen: The Ancient Sun Kingdoms of the Americas)

I weep
for a people
without name
who chiselled me

from a cage
of stone
in the childhood
of their culture

who heaped my altar
with gifts of flesh
and gold
who lay trembling before me

when their sunlight
faltered
who measured time
against shadow

who loved to dance
who imagined my lava tears
were shed
to nourish maize

whose fate
my blank eyes had surveyed
condensing
in the land of the Inca

I weep
for the anvil-headed clouds
weightlessly approaching
beautifully darkening

and I weep in the prison
of my omniscience
for all I foresaw
but had not the power to change

## Above Pennan

*fragment of earth*
*fragment of moon*
*memory of flesh*
*memory of bone*

    corn heads
    heavy and luminous
    listless as water
    stirred by the night wind
    night moon

*memory of flesh*
*memory of bone*
*fragment of earth*
*fragment of moon*

    hush
    beyond the field's edge
    the old workings
    of the hidden sea
    jealous for land

*fragment of earth*
*fragment of moon*
*memory of flesh*
*memory of bone*

    across the unfocussed acres
    of the night
    the layered dead
    unfurl
    in whispers

*memory of flesh*
*memory of bone*
*fragment of earth*
*fragment of moon*

# The House At Boreraig

*after Reinhard Behrens*

I'll not go to the house at Boreraig.
I've no desire to watch the stones
resign their gradual geometry;

and there's no comfort for me
in the song of the rowan, as it empties
the old seasons from its frame.

Instead, I'll wear these
tokens fixed to my conscience
like dead stoats on a fence:

1.   a riddled copper bowl
     which bleeds in the late rain;

2.   a twist of barbed wire
     clogged with oily fleece;

3.   an eroded bread knife;

4.   a curl of bootsole,
     smoothed by a child's foot; and

5.   by the twisted lock,
     of the broken door,
     of the tumbled wall,
     of the burned house of Boreraig;
     a key, infinitesimally
     turning in its hidden grave.

# A Man

Somewhere else,
he has a wife
who has not always
been so quiet,
or so grey.

How she adores
the photographs
of her children.

She worships their smiling
constancy as the great hours
drift like dust into her hands,
and the faithful clock
unwinds towards
silence.

## Coal

Coal glistens in the mirk of our cellar.
I smell its bitter breath where it squats in a corner,

Like a condemned man, bent on martyrdom.
This resignation fuels our summer.

Through the midstream swirl of winter,
In our dim cupola of firelight,

We shall watch the helpless struggles of an orange bird
Fluttering in a gin of ashes,

From which, he must know, he can never be freed.
And our palms will glow with his despair.

# Coffee Spoons

*'The days of our age are threescore years and ten;'*
(Psalms 90:10)

I'm thirty three this year;
but I don't really understand time; it's too twiddly.
Now, if my life were pennies,
and I mean real pennies—those copper discs
once placed in telephones and people's eyes—
if my life were pennies, then I would be two and ninepence.
That's not much; not these days,
but it means I've squandered almost half my five and ten.

Thirty three inches.
Almost three feet, and I should live until
I'm just under six feet, before I'm six feet under.
I make that another three feet one inch I'm still due.
The sunlight, crawling through the darkness of my room,
could cover that in something like an hour.

Thirty three ounces.
2lbs 1oz.
Four potatoes and a carrot.
I can visualise that.
In another five potatoes I'll be 4lb 6ozs;
a scrawny infant carried wailing to the grave.

Thirty three degrees fahrenheit.
That's not quite ice: that's a Fort William spring.
But I'm only going as far as Bognor Regis in early June.

Thirty three miles per hour.
Think about it.
You might notice the heads turn in the jam sandwich
as you cruise along the High Street,
on the far side of legality.
And seventy?
Seventy is only another street away,
all lateral details blurred;

43

the right foot pressed hard against the floor,
and just enough time left to glance in the rear-view
mirror, and marvel at how smoothly
and how fast
the pursuing blue light grows to fill the glass.

# The Bright Cloud

*after Samuel Palmer*

What fragment of
eternity will he find with her,
concealed between
the scent of hay
and darkness; where
the movement
of a hand might silence
for one stroke the heartbeat
of oblivion;
where her embrace
encompasses the sunlit heights,
the distant rain?

## Second-hand Books

Old books
encompass subtler books, worked
without language.

Scorning the bland
materialism of the pressed flower, they convey
scent without bloom.

To read these books
is to wear the twill trousers
of the dead—

to struggle with unfamiliar
buttons, then suffer the disquiet
of a perfect fit.

Their pungency breathes
of dim leached souls, whom forked
words led astray.

How faithfully each
yellowed page translates the smoke of pine;
the lavender

and paraffin; the moist
air drifting from untended walls.
Such musty perfume

lures me from the lines
of ink—those strands of darkness where
all meaning falls away.

Helpless as dust, I drift
towards the light, the luminous, the lucid.
The sweet lack of words.

# Wet Roofs

*after Bill Brandt*

A flight of gables climbs the buried hill.
The wet slates flare against the quartzy light,
and lead the eye towards a shadowed yard,

with its line of washing sagged by laundering rain.
Someone, somewhere inside those huddled
terraces, believed this rain would cease.

Beyond the line, a single window hangs distinct;
its faded curtains only partly drawn.
That soiled shape lurking by the astragal

could be a mirror, or a cracked jug,
or a face. Somewhere there must be people;
somewhere, unfathomed people; watching their

moments break against a sky as ponderous
as smoke; watching the persistent rain weigh down
upon the strings of houses, and the linen

moored to stone; watching daylight slip
from the glass; and their own reflections rise up
like muslin on the far side of their lives.

## Making Things Dark

A dark wind lifts
the pages from my desk,
and scatters them through the open window
to the pine woods,
and the unlit fields.
These is no point in chasing after them.
I go back to my desk and begin again.

The shadow of the poem
darkens the paper.
The meaning darkens
in the shadow of the word.
Time absolves me
from the burden of the truth.

Why do I write? I write
to weight the pages
of my life.
I write to give the shadows depth.
Why do I write?
I write to make things dark.

*FROM AN OCCUPIED COUNTRY*

# Red Shift

Sunsets are spectacular
these days. Our skin burns painlessly
in the fly-sprung twilight.

When salmon flesh droops
crimson for the knife, we remember
the hanging poacher's blood,

slicker than asphalt.
Those small mountain poppies,
fragile as butterflies,

tremble in their cyanotic
beauty. Philosophers detachedly
remove the petals, saying,

*"Beauty is enhanced by transience."*
The Physicists agree.
They have deduced

from blemishes upon the skeleton
of light, that something is leaving
our world.

# *The End Of The Hot Water Bottles*

It had to come.
Time rubbed her yellow
toenails on the bags so often
that the little perishers gave up

the ghost in unison, that winter's night.
A suppurating lung oozed at the foot
of every bed. No one stirred as they
leached their contents

through the sheets,
cosy as urine;
but the next day,
glue-eyed and dopey,

we shivered in our freshly
recollected guilt, like children
who rise from a common dream, baffled
by the sudden vision of a world blown huge.

# The Song Of The Woolly Mammoth

I remember how the pressure
of your belly bleached the grass.
In the photograph your eyes

appeared half closed.
I remember the smell of your spine, bruised
by the weight of darkness—

those craneflies
wearing out their little engines
on our wall.

I remember how you idly
swung your legs. The shadow of leaves
against a page.

You said they had found
a frozen mammoth in the tundra.
Fresh clover in its jaws.

## *Typography*

At the presses, they grumble constantly
about the quality of ink; although this makes
the books more difficult to burn.
No fresh types issue from the rook-filled

foundries. Old characters are wearing back
towards ancestral runes.
The newspapers no longer convey information,
but generate a speculative philosophy

based on rumour, and the size of type.
The poor malnourished printers suffer dreadfully
with hacks. They tell us how painful
they find it, touching those long words.

# Dog Days

We turned them loose
when food reserves were
almost done. Poor dogs.
Torn between hunger
and the memory of love,
they hung around until
the stones began to fall,
then slunk off to the mountains,
growing thin and sly.

This winter, when they hauled
our screaming baby from its pram,
or snatched the chickens from their open coop,
they sloped back to the woods
reluctantly, almost apologetically.

They'll soon forget our smell
now that their rotting collars
have worked free.
But strangely, in the hollow
of the night, we often
hear the guide dogs
howling in their dreadful freedom.

# *Pottery*

Grandfather collects potsherds
from ploughed fields behind the house.
Spring rain has made them gleam.

He says he cannot recall
whose fingers shaped the clay,
but each year pieces stubbornly

return, in lessening diameters.
Now he lines his room with tesserae
from their past. Bottle bottoms crook

the green light in a corner window.
Segments of pipe stem litter the coffee
table like the shattered ribs of some

extinct marsupial. He hands me
a splinter of oriental plate, where
a stranded lover waits

on a fractured bridge.
"*Someone, someday,*" he says,
"*Will watch our lives go down like this.*"

## A Difficult Colour

Think of it this way.
Imagine a sea voyage. You have drawn

the boat up on the shingle for the night.
The water is barely luminous.

Someone points into the gloom. On the far hill
they are burning crofts.

The rain comes on again, but softly,
to preserve the sanctity of desecration.

You stand watching the reflections
tremble upon the water.

It's that sort of colour.

## Precarious Days

The mackerel tribe is shy
this year. Winds rise,
boats sink, bellies rumble.
Each night the sootfalls

gather in our empty hearth.
I use saliva to mix ink
out of fire, then char the backs
of envelopes with my dreams.

Our womenfolk are talking
quietly about the visitors
from the South. Moss thrives
on my favourite slippers.

# The Star

We followed the fallen star,
and dug out a cooling fist of stone
that gleamed like armour
in our hands. Later we drove on
towards the looted town.

Beside the byre, a bound man
with his throat ripped.
Bloodstained straw.
His 'wife or daughter
huddled in the corner,
beaten and defiled.

What could we do?
Her time was near,
and so for warmth,
we wrapped her innocence
around our star.

Beyond the door
the night sky glimmered
with the flowerings of distant war.
We slept in an open courtyard,
woke to the rain.
Meanwhile, death struggled
from the virgin's womb,
smiling with pain.

# A Traditional Curse

When apoplexy
strikes, may you
not die.

May you revive
beneath a calm sky,
hanging larks,

freshly stamped turf.
May you retain
the breath to cry out

strongly; tasting
stale air
which dribbles

from your box
like colourless
sand.

And may somebody
lingering close by
hear you. The fool

whose village your burned,
picking earth
from his nails.

## Strange Diseases

*"comprising well differentiated tissue*

*primitive*
*bone and hair*

*the pseudofoetus, or 'invasive cystoid',*
*grows rapidly within the colon*
*of the adult male*

*ten centimeters. The sub-mucous*
*pedicle detaches spontaneously*
*and the growth is expelled,*
*with some discomfort,*
*in the normal manner.*

*Occasionally rudimentary eyes*
*and limb buds can be seen."*

They told us not to drink the water.
Women call the cysts 'Virgin's Revenge.'
They giggle as we squat and groan.
The excreted matter is burned
or flushed.
Our village butcher took it really bad.
Two days in his toilet, till they
booted down the door.
He was sitting weeping with the floppy
cancer in his hands.
Said he had felt sure
it was alive;
clumsily holding on.

# The Crossing

We pushed on the next day.
It was a hard slog, following the track
beside the grey river. Some of us
flagged a bit; I began coughing,
and spat red in the palm of my hand.

There was a young girl dropped
her child too soon.
The still foetus steamed at the edge
of a frozen field. We didn't pause
to count the fingers.
No witnesses to the mewling death
but ourselves, and a plague horse
with bloated stomach sagging
beneath a tree.

The crows were bold, because
it was a bitter summer.
When we reached the broken town,
fires everywhere;
you could almost touch the stench
of burning dogs. A crossbow bolt
took out one of the slower men
as we jogged to cover. No one dared go back
to fetch his clothes.

That night we smelled the salt
air in the breeze,
and comforted ourselves
with talk of a gentle crossing
on calm seas.
They had said the Government
had full control on the other side.
There would be plenty food
so long as we could work.
The Forces there had everything in hand.

At dawn we set off, trudging
in silence until we saw the ocean,
then chatting and laughing incautiously;
made brave by its proximity.
There had been snow,
but the day brightened
as we reached the shore.

A little boat lay tied up
on the shingle and a blind man
was drawing his nets from the grey water.
We asked about the crossing,
but he shook his head:

*'We only escaped by the skin of our arses.*
*They did this to me for fun.'*
(He pulled up his wrinkled
eyelids from their empty sockets.)

Some of us helped him with the nets.
A scant catch of stunted flatfish
flapped their warped spines
in a last despair.
We moved on the next day.

# A Science Fiction Story

Embodiments or projections?
We couldn't tell, but they existed
as shadows in shackled energy;
a bell of effervescent air.

The spectra of cataracts rose
endlessly around them, seeking
invisibility in a stench of ozone.
We sensed the tang of metal on our tongues.

In humorous music-hall jargon,
they described their parent world.
We watched the rain dimple and streak
the mud around their cage.

They said they had come to tell us
how our world would end.
We already knew.
They demonstrated therapeutic instruments

beyond our comprehension.
We considered abandoning the wheel.
They said they had not understood
they were too late. We signed

against the evil eye, turning for home.
Weeks later they persisted, translucent
and uncertain, wearing masks of rain;
but in the end, they faded back to gods again.

# Goodbye

Goodbye to you in your range rovers.
Goodbye in your carts, on your
donkeys, and your blistered feet.
Goodbye to our finest corn,
our fattest cattle,

our hamstrung children.
When you pause to look back,
our eyes turn to salt,
seeing such wealth removed
from the belly of our land.

Goodbye to our full bellies.
When you are long away,
we will thank you for the single gift
you left behind—the spare
constraints of your tongue.

Those thin vowels and ashy consonants
are crumbling to nothing in our mouths.
Thank you for your good language,
which you taught us so that
we might understand goodbye.